Fish, Milk,Tamarind

T0352281

Fish, Milk, Tamarind

A Book of Egyptian Arabic
Food Expressions

Dalal Abo El Seoud

Illustrated by Farah Shafie

The American University in Cairo Press
Cairo   New York

First published in 2022 by
The American University in Cairo Press
113 Sharia Kasr el Aini, Cairo, Egypt
One Rockefeller Plaza, 10th Floor, New York, NY 10020
www.aucpress.com

ISBN 978 1 649 03190 7

Library of Congress Cataloging-in-Publication Data

Names: Abo El Seoud, Dalal Yassin, author. | Shafie, Farah, illustrator.
Title: Fish, milk, tamarind : a book of Egyptian Arabic food expressions / Dalal Abo El Seoud ; illustrated by Farah Shafie.
Identifiers: LCCN 2021043231 | ISBN 9781649031907 (hardback)
Subjects: LCSH: Arabic language--Dialects--Egypt--Terms and phrases. | Arabic language—Terms and phrases. | Arabic language--Egypt--Idioms. |Food--Terminology.
Classification: LCC PJ6779 .A26 2021 | DDC 492.7/70962--dc23/eng/20211013

1 2 3 4 5   26 25 24 23 22

Designed by David G. Hanna
Printed in China

I dedicate this book to my lovely family,

My husband,
My children, and
My grandchildren

INTRODUCTION

Fish, Milk, Tamarind: While the meaning of the title of this book may confuse the non-native reader, its Egyptian Arabic translation makes up a popular expression used to describe a mishmash of things that are lacking in harmony or consistency. This book brings together one hundred commonly used Egyptian food expressions and sayings, covering a wide range of meanings and uses.

Idiomatic expressions are fascinating and fun. They lend color, dynamism, and humor to everyday speech, and convey complex ideas and beliefs with an economy of words that tell us something about the culture from which they spring.

As an Arabic-language instructor, I often find that non-native learners of the language seldom get exposed to everyday expressions and sayings in their textbooks, and therefore have little opportunity to use or understand them in their day-to-day communication with native speakers.

Adding expressions like the ones in this book to one's speech can raise cultural awareness and help learners of Arabic to listen out for other expressions as well as work out the implied meaning behind them based on context. This awareness helps learners build and sustain their linguistic and cultural development.

I chose food as my theme because eating is an important communal event in Egyptian homes, and since they are also closely tied to cooking and cuisine, the expressions in this book can tell us something about the relative importance of certain foods in Egyptian culture and the kinds of meanings associated with them.

The idiomatic expressions listed in this book are so deeply embedded in the culture that they are often used by native speakers almost unconsciously, to express points of view that do not necessarily adhere strictly to their literal meanings. For instance, one might argue that a person who describes a woman as being زَيّ الْمَلْبَـن (which literally translates to "like Turkish delight") simply means to say that she is "lovely."

Deeper analysis of some of these expressions, however, may serve to strip them of their seeming innocence and invite us to reexamine the purpose they serve when employed in everyday speech.

The expressions are accompanied by delightful illustrations, which also serve as helpful memory aids for learners. Each entry includes the original word, phrase, or sentence in Arabic, its English transcription, and its meanings in English, both literal and intended.

Arabic learners of all levels, from elementary to advanced, as well as heritage learners of the language can benefit from this book, while native speakers and lovers of Egypt will find much in it to delight and entertain them.

May it serve as a source of learning and joy!

TRANSCRIPTION LIST

This is a list to help you pronounce the transcription of the expressions provided in this book.

- **Long vowels:**
  aa: Sounds like the /a/ vowel in the English word "fan"
  ee: Sounds like the /a/ vowel in the English word "fair"
  ii: Sounds like the /ee/ vowels in the English word "feet"
  oo: Sounds like the /o/ vowel in the English word "note"
  uu: Sounds like the /oo/ vowels in the English word "spoon"

- **Short vowels:**
  a: Sounds like the /a/ vowel in English word "maybe"
  e/i: Sounds like the /i/ in the English word "fig"
  o/u: Sounds like the /o/ in the English word "to"

- **Emphatic sounds:**
  Always written in English capital letters to differentiate them from their ordinary English-like counterparts (note that Arabic has no capital letters).
  S: Sounds like the /su/ sound in the English word "sun"
  D: Sounds like the /da/ sound in the English word "dawn"
  T: Sounds like the /tu/ sound in the English word "tummy"

4. **The glottal stop:**

': This indicates a glottal stop. Although it is not an English letter, you will find it pronounced twice in the English expression "uh-oh," before the u, and before the o. It is used here to represent two different letters in Arabic. For the purpose of simplicity, I will not differentiate between them here since they are pronounced exactly the same.

Sounds not found in English:

kh: Sounds as if you are scratching your throat. It is also the snoring sound. This is a fricative voiceless velar sound. Voiceless means that it does not need the vocal cords to produce the sound. It is articulated from the following place:

gh: This sounds like the gurgling sound, or the French "r" sound. It is a fricative voiced velar sound. Voiced means that the vocal cords are needed to produce this letter. It is articulated from the following place:

Notice that it is articulated from the same point as the "kh" but one is voiceless and the other is voiced.

H: This is the sound that you make when you eat hot chili peppers! It is pronounced further back from the English /h/ sound. It is a fricative voiceless pharyngeal sound (does not require the work of the vocal cords to produce it). It is articulated from the following place:

ع: This sounds like the sound you make when "throwing up." It is not found in English; this is why I have kept it in its Arabic form. It comes from the same place as the one above, /H/, but requires the work of the vocal cords for producing it. It is a fricative voiced pharyngeal sound. It is articulated from the following place.

Practice placing your fingers on your throat to produce the voiceless /H/ and the voiced /ع/. All other letters in the expressions in this book sound exactly like their English counterparts.

Final note: Doubled consonants indicate a sound is pronounced twice. An example in English would be the double k sound in "bookcase."

Expressions

زَيِّ الْعَسَل

zayyil ع asal

(Like honey)

A very sweet or nice person

(or thing)

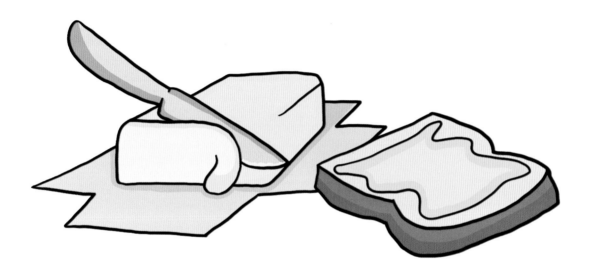

زَيِّ الزِّبْدَة

zayyiz zibda

(Like butter)

Very lean

(food)

زَيِّ الرُّز

zayyir ruzz

(Like rice)

A lot of, an abundance of

(things or people)

زَيِّ الْقِشْطَة

zayyil 'ishTa

(Like cream)

A very beautiful woman

(usually with fair skin)

زَيِّ الْمَلْبَن

zayyil malban

(Like Turkish delight)

Soft and flexible (things) or soft and plump (women)

زَيِّ اللُّوز

zayyil looz

(Like almonds)

When food looks very fresh

زَيِّ الْبَسْكُوتَة

zayyil baskuuta

(Like a biscuit)

A very delicate

(person or thing)

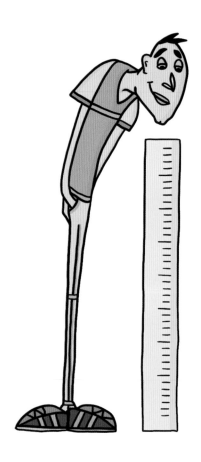

زَيِّ عُود الْقَصَب

zayyi عuud il'aSab

(Like a stalk of sugar cane)

Someone who's

tall and thin

زَيِّ السِّكِّينَة فِي الْحَلاوَة

zayyis skkiina fil Halaawa

(Like a knife cutting through halva)

Smooth and easy

زَيِّ السُّكَر

zayyis sukkar

(Like sugar)

A very sweet or nice person

(or thing)

زَيِّ الشَّرْبَات

zayyish sharbaat

(Like sharbaat (a type of sweet, flavored drink))

A very sweet or nice

person (or thing)

قَرْع

'are

(Pumpkin)

Lying or fabrication

بُونْبُونَايَة

bunbunaaya

(A piece of candy)

A sweet, lovely person

سَلَطَة

SalaTa

(Salad)

A mess

سَمْن عَلَى عَسَل

samna ع ala ع asal

(Ghee with honey)

They're living harmoniously together

أَنَا مَيَّه / شُورْبَة

'ana mayya / shorba

(I'm water/soup)

I'm sweating excessively

كُوسَة/خِيَار وفَقُّوس

kuusa / khiyaar wi fa''uus

(Zucchini / Cucumber and gourd)

Nepotism

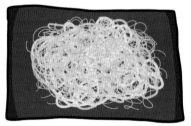

كُنَافَة

kunaafa

(A dessert made of shredded phyllo pastry)

Something complicated

مِتْقَمَّع

mit'amma3

(Okra with its top sliced off)

Dressed to the nines

حَاجَة مُوز

Haaga mooz

(It's bananas)

Something that's very good

نَايمة فِي الْعَسَل

nayma fil ع asal

(Sleeping in honey)

Someone who's oblivious

فِي الْمِشْمِش

fil mishmish

(in the apricots)

It will never happen

قِشْطَة

'ishTa

(Cream!)

Cool! Let's do it!

وِشُّه زَيِّ اللَّمُونَة

wishshu zayyil lamuuna

(His face is like a lemon)

His skin looks very pale/sickly

فُولَة وِاتْقَسَمِت نُصِّين

fuula wit'asamit nuSSeen

(A broad bean split in two)

Two people who are very alike

خُدُودْهَا زَيِّ التُّفَاح

khududha zayyit tuffaaH

(Her cheeks are like apples)

She has rosy cheeks

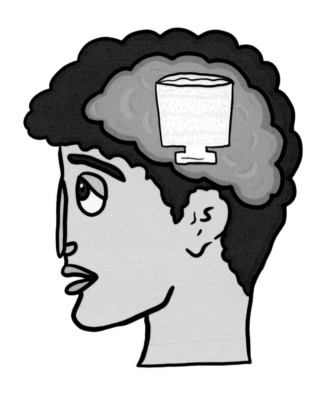

مُخُّه مِهَلَّبِيَّة

mukhkhu mhallabiyya

(His brain is milk pudding)

He's simpleminded

مِسَمْسِم

misamsim

(Covered in sesame seeds)

He has small, cute features

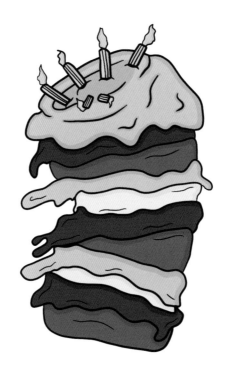

كُفْتَة

kufta

(Meatballs)

Sloppy work

بَقِت خَل

ba'it khal

(It turned into vinegar)

Things have deteriorated

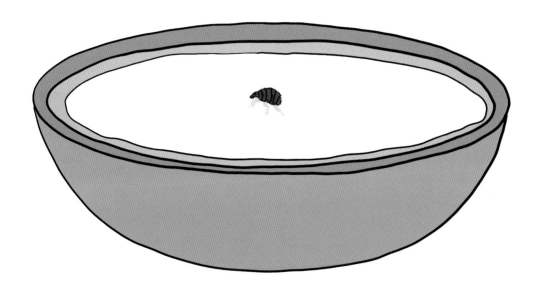

زَيِّ الْبَرْغُوت فِي اللَّبَن

zayyil barغuut fil laban

(Like a flea in milk)

Something that's very obvious

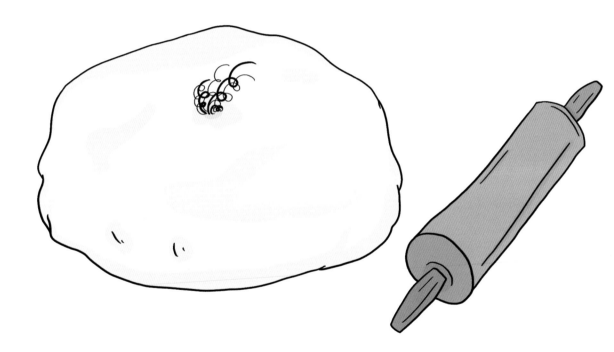

زَيِّ الشَّعْرَة من الْعَجِينَة

zayyish sha؏ra mil ؏agiina

(Like a hair from dough)

Someone who managed to escape

the consequences of a situation

الْعَدَد فِي اللَّمُون

ilₑadad fil lamuun

(The number is in the lemons)

Something that is abundant

and low in value

رَقَبْتُه بَقِت قَدِّ السِّمْسِمَة

ra'abtu ba'it addis simsima

(His neck shrank to the size of a sesame seed)

He felt humiliated

حُطَّ فِي بَطْنَك بَطّيخَة صِيفِي

HuTTif baTnak baTTiikha Seefi

(Put a summer watermelon in your stomach)

Don't worry at all

اِنْقَعْهَا وِاشْرَب مَيِّتْهَا

'in'aعha wishrab mayyitha

(Soak it and drink its water)

It's useless

تِبْقَى فِي بُقَّك وِتِقْسَم لِغيرَك

tib'af bu''ak wi ti'sam ligheerak

(It was already in your mouth, then someone else took it)

You were very close to winning something,

but it turns out to be meant for someone else

لَبَن الْعَصْفُور

laban عaSfuur

(Bird's milk)

**Something that will
never be found**

عَمَل مِن الْحَبَّة قُبَّة

ع*amal mil Habba 'ubba*

(To make a mountain out of a seed)

To make a mountain out of a molehill

ميَّه من تَحْت تِبْن

mayya min taHti tibn

(Water under hay)

A snake in the grass

لَاقِينِي وَ لَا تِغَدِّينِي

la'iini walat ghaddiini

(Give me a warm welcome rather than offering me lunch)

A warm welcome is the most

important thing

كَلْ عَلَيَّ فْلُوسِي

kal ع alayya fluusi

(He ate my money)

He conned me

أنا اتْشَوِيت

'ana 'itshaweet

(I've been grilled)

I got sunburned

بِيَاكُل رُزْ مَعَ الْمَلَايْكَة

biyaakul ruzzi maعal malayka

(He's eating rice with the angels)

He's fast asleep

عَصَرِت عَلَى نَفْسَها لَمُونَة

ع aSarit ع ala nafsaha lamuuna

(She squeezed a lemon on herself)

She controlled her anger

أَكْل عِيش

'akli ع eesh

(Eating bread)

Making a living

كَلْنَا مَعَ بَعْض عِيش وِمَلْح

kalna maɛa baɛD ɛeesh wi malH

(We ate bread and salt together)

We've been through a lot together

زَيِّ عِلْبِة السَّرْدِين

zayyi ع ilbitis sardiin

(Like a tin of sardines)

Very crowded

مَا تِتْبَلِّش فِي بُقُّه فُولَة

ma titballish fi bu'u fuula

(A bean wouldn't get wet in his mouth)

He can't keep a secret

عَمَل مَعَايَا الْجُلَّاشَة

ع*amal ma*عـ *aayal gullaasha*

(He made gullaash (a phyllo meat pie) with me)

He tricked / deceived me

وِشُّه بَقَى زَيِّ الطَّمَاطْمَايَة

wishshu ba'a zayyiT TamaTmaaya

(His face turned into a tomato)

He's blushing

بِيِغْرَق فِي شِبْرِ مَيَّه

biyiɣra' fishibri mayya

(He drowns in a few inches of water)

He becomes confused very quickly,

can't manage anything by himself

وِشُّه قَدِّ اللُّقْمَة

wishshu 'addil lu'ma

(His face is as small as a bite of bread)

His face has become extremely thin

(due to illness or diet)

صَام صَام وِفِطِر عَلَى بَصَلَة

Saam Saam wifiTir عala baSala

(He fasted and fasted, then broke his fast with an onion)

After all his efforts, he didn'tget

the result he was hoping for

قَارِش مَلْحِتِي

'aarish malHiti

(He's crunching my grain of salt)

He understands my tricks

يِعْمِل مِن الْفِسِيخ شَرْبَات

yiεmil milfisiikh sharbaat

(To make sugar syrup from rotten fish)

To make something good

out of something bad

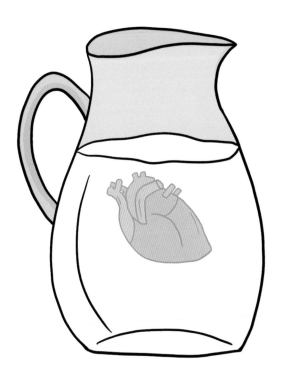

قَلْبُه زَيِّ اللَّبَن الْحَلِيب

'albu zayyil laban ilHaliib

(His heart is like milk)

He's very kind, has no hard

feelings towards anyone

رَاح فِي شَرْبِة مَيَّه

raaH fi sharbit mayya

(He was lost in a drink of water)

He was seriously harmed as a result of something seemingly small or innocuous

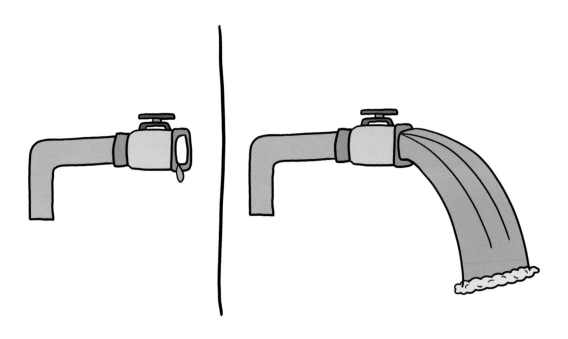

رِجْعِت الْمَيَّه لِمَجَارِيهَا

rigɛitil mayyal magariiha

(The water returned to its natural course)

Things went back to normal

وَجَع الْبَطْن وَلَا كَبِّ الطَّبِيخ

wagaε il baTni walla kabbiT Tabiikh

(Having a stomachache is better than throwing away food)

Overeating is better than

throwing away leftovers

بِيِلْعَب بِالْبِيَضة واِلْحَجَر

biyilعab bil beeDa wil Hagar

(He's playing with eggs and stones)

He's a con artist

يَاكُل وِينْكِر

yaakul wiyinkir

(He eats and denies it)

He's never grateful

حَاخَلِّيهَا لَك كَحْكَة

Ha khallihaalak kaHka

(I'll turn it into a cookie for you)

I'll make it very beautiful

حِتّة لَحْمَة حَمْرَا

Hittit laHma Hamra

(A piece of red meat)

A baby

نَاكُلْهَا بِدُقَّة

nakulha bdu''a

(We'll eat it with dukka (a simple spice-and-nut mix))

We'll make do with

what we have

لِسَانْهَا بِيْنَقَّط سُكَّر

lisanha biyna''aT sukkar

(Sugar drips from her tongue)

She uses pleasant

and gentle words

سَمَك لَبَن تَمْر هِنْدِي

samak laban tamrihindi

(Fish, milk, and tamarind)

**A mishmash of things that
don't go together at all**

سَلْق بِيض

sal'i beeD

(Boiling eggs)

Doing something hastily

and carelessly

زَيِّ اللُّقْمَة فِي الزُّور

zayyil lu'ma fizzoor

(Like food stuck in the throat)

A pain in the neck

اللِّي مَا بِعْرَفْش يُقُول عَدْس

'illi mayiعrafsh yi'uul عads

(Anyone who doesn't know says "lentils")

If someone doesn't know something,

s/he would give any response

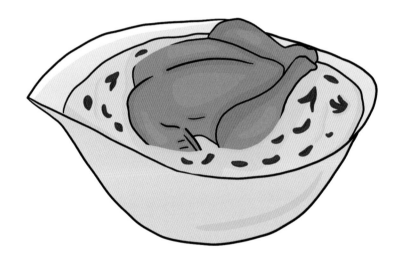

فَرْخَة بْكِشْك

farkha bkishk

(Chicken with kishk (a creamy dip))

An excellent opportunity

مَفِيش حَلَاوَة مِن غِير نار

mafiish Halaawa min gheer naar

(There is no dessert without fire)

You can't achieve something

worthwhile without some loss/effort

(you can't make an omelet without breaking eggs)

بَصَلِة الْمُحِبِّ خَرُوف

baSalitil muHibbi kharuuf

(An onion from a lover tastes like lamb)

Anything that comes from

a beloved feels valuable

عَمَل مِن الْبَحْر طِحِينَة

ɛamal mil baHri THiina

(He turned the sea into tahini)

**He's exaggerating
something greatly**

كَل وِشِّي

kal wishshi

(He ate my face)

He embarassed me

طَالِع وَاكِل نَازِل وَاكِل

Taaliɛ waakil naazil waakil

(He's eating on his way up and on his way down)

Someone who's opportunistic

or exploitative

نِتْغَدَّى بِيه قَبْلِ مَا يِتْعَشَّى بِينَا

nitغadda biih 'ablima yitغashsha biina

(Let's eat him for lunch before he eats us for dinner)

Let's get him before he gets us

مِش كُلِّ طِير يِتَّاكِل لَحْمُه

mish kulli Teer yittaakil laHmu

(One cannot eat the meat of any bird)

**If you're strong, no one
can harm you**

دِي مُوزَة مَقَشَّرَة

di mooza m'ashshara

(It's a peeled banana)

This is an excellent opportunity

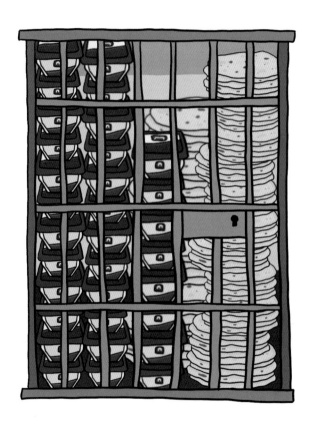

حَاجِيب لَك عِيش وِحَلَاوَة

Hagib lak ع eesh wiHalaawa

(I'll bring you bread and halva)

The person addressed

will be in trouble

إِنْ كَان حَبِيبَك عَسَل مَا تِلْحَسُوش كُلُّه

'in kan Habiibak ع asal matilHasuush kullu

(If your beloved is made of honey, don't lick him/her all up)

If your loved one is kind,

don't take advantage of him/her

الدِّهْن فِي الْعَتَاقِي

'iddihn fil ع ataa'i

(The fat is in the older ones)

**Older people have
more experience**

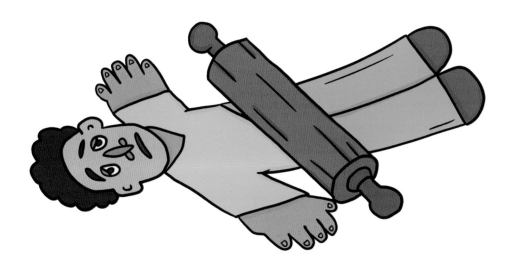

عَجْنَاه وخَبْزَاه

عagnaa w khabzaa

(I've kneaded and baked him)

I know him inside out

اللِّي يَاكُل عَلَى ضِرْسُه يِنْفَع نَفْسُه

'illi yaakul ع ala Dirsu yinfa ع nafsu

(The one who eats on his own molar benefits him/herself)

You need to take care of

your own needs

وِدْن مِن طِين وِوِدْن مِن عَجِين

widni min Tiin wiwidni min عagiin

(One ear is made of mud and the other of dough)

To turn a deaf ear

أَكْلِ وْمَرْعَى وِقِلِّة صَنْعَة

'akli wmarعa wi'llit Sanعa

(food, pasture, and no work)

Someone who's lying around,

relaxing and not being productive

أَنَا اِتْفَرَمْت / أَنَا اِسْتَوِيت / أَنا مَهْرِيَّة / أَنَا مَعْجُونَة

'ana maₑguuna / 'ana mahriyya / anas taweet / anat faramt

(I've been kneaded, I'm cooked, I'm overcooked, I've been ground like meat)

I'm exhausted

عِنَب

ɛinab

(Grapes)

Great!

يَا حَلاوَة

ya Halaawa!

(Oh halva!)

Oh really?!

(with sarcasm)

فَصٌّ مَلْح ودَاب

faSSi malHiw daab

(A grain of salt that has dissolved)

Something (or someone)

that has vanished

بَلَح

balaH

(Dates)

Something that's fake or untrue

إِدِّي الْعِيش لِخَبَّازُه وَلَوْ كَلْ نُصُّه

'idil ع eesh likhabbaazu wi law kal nuSSu

(Give the bread to its baker even if he eats half of it)

Assign tasks to those who have

the skills even if they are expensive

طَبَّاخ السِّمِّ بِيْدُوقُه

Tabbaakh issim biyduu'u

(The one who prepares poison will get a taste of it)

What goes around comes around

اللِّي اِتْلَسَع مِن الشُّورْبَة يُنْفُخ فِي الزَّبَادِي

'illit lasaع mishshurba yunfukh fizzabaadi

(Those who get their tongues burned by soup will blow on yogurt to cool it down)

Once burned, twice shy

تَاكْلِي صَوَابْعِك وَرَاها

takli Sawabعik waraha

(You (f.) eat your fingers after it)

It is delicious

بِتْلِتِّ وْتِعْجِن

bitlittiw tiɛgin

(She's pouring water on the flour and kneading it)

She's rambling on

about something

طِلِع مِن الْمُولِدِ بِلَا حُمُّص

Tiliع mil muulid bila HummuS

(He came out of the festival without chickpeas)

He came out of a potentially profitable

situation with nothing to show for it

مَطْلِعْش مِن الْبِيضَة

maTliɛ shi mil beeDa

(He hasn't hatched out of the egg)

He's young and inexperienced

لُقْمِة الْعِيش

lu'mitil ع eesh

(A bite of bread)

Making a living

اِتْغَدَّى بِيه قَبْلِ ما يِتْعَشَّى بِيك

'itغadda biih 'ablima yitعashsha biik

(Eat him for lunch before he eats you for dinner)

Kill him before he kills you